Ripley's Believe It or Not!

Amusement Park Oddities & Trivia!

A Journey Through the WEIRD, Wacky, and *Absolutely True*
World of Parks, Rides, and Attractions

by TIM O'BRIEN • • • illustrations by JOHN GRAZIANO

*"When I am called a liar by a reader of my cartoons,
I feel flattered because it means to me that my cartoon
that day contained some strange fact that was
unbelievable — and therefore most interesting, and
that the reader did not know the truth when he saw it!"*

- ROBERT RIPLEY, 1929

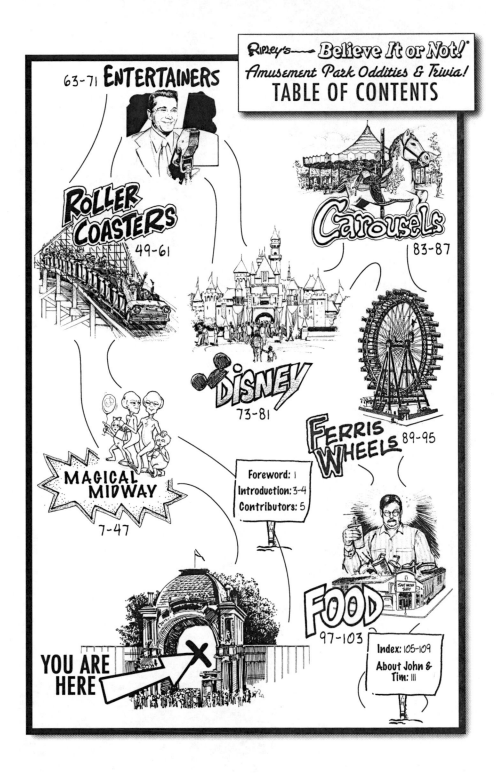

Ripley's ——— Believe *It or Not!*
Amusement Park Oddities & Trivia!
TABLE OF CONTENTS

Foreword

When Tim O'Brien came to me with the idea of creating a Believe It or Not! book on amusement parks, rides and attractions, it didn't take me long to agree.

During 75 years of book publishing, our company has published specialty books on everything from sports to sea life, but never on the industry in which we as a company specialize - visitor attractions! I felt it was time!

With a bit of history, a bit of trivia and a lot of totally unbelievable facts, this is a first of its kind book for our industry. After reading the manuscript, I truly agree that this is definitely a "journey through the weird, wacky and absolutely true world of amusement park oddities and trivia."

Thinking that a cowboy figure that served as a prop in a dark ride was a wax figure only to find out decades later that it was a real human body – weird!

Finding out that Knute Rockne perfected the forward pass on the beaches of Cedar Point where he was employed as a lifeguard – amazing!

That Elvis Presley's last public appearance was at an all night coaster-riding outing in Memphis – incredible!

That Cannon Ball the dog lived under a coaster and followed it each time it left the station, running 326,592 laps during his life – wacky.

And that's just a sampling. There are hundreds more of these great little nuggets. Enjoy!

Bob Masterson – President, Ripley Entertainment

Introduction

Robert Ripley coined one of the most familiar American lexicons, "Believe It or Not! nearly 90 years ago as the name for his popular cartoon panel of the odd and unusual. The distinctive style and the bizarre content made the cartoon a huge success. Today, as the world's oldest daily comic, it is still read in nearly 200 newspapers in 42 different countries!

Through the years, to gather information for his popular cartoon and later for his Believe It or Not! odditoriums, Ripley became an intrepid world traveler. He brought back amazing and weird stories, artifacts, and illustrations, most of which we still have in our 30-plus odditoriums throughout the world today.

What I have always appreciated about Ripley's Believe It or Not! is that everything presented is true and genuine! Ripley took great pride in presenting things so preposterous that their accuracy was immediately questioned. He was proven wrong only a handful of times through the years.

Since Ripley's death in 1949, the caretakers of his legacy and his archives have followed suit and have presented the best of the weird, strange, uncanny, creepy and bizarre facts and artifacts - all genuine and true - to the worlds curious.

In keeping with the Ripley tradition, the information in this book, the first Ripley's Believe It or Not! publication dedicated to amusement parks, theme parks, rides and attractions, is true and genuine to the best of our knowledge. Many industry eyes have confirmed and reconfirmed the odd and unusual material presented here.

Within the pages of this little book, you'll find more than 350 fun, unbelievable, and often odd and bizarre facts and stories and more than 50 amazing, original illustrations by Ripley's official illustrator, John Graziano. In addition, I've worked in a few "Ripley's Classics" that Robert Ripley himself drew prior to 1949.

From bums eating nickel hot dogs at Coney Island, to the beaches of Cedar Point, to a park within a cave in the Artic Circle in Finland, you'll discover the quirky side of the amusement industry. It will be revealed directly in front of you that truth is definitely more bizarre and stranger than fiction! Enjoy!

Tim O'Brien, AUTHOR, IS VP PUBLISHING & COMMUNICATIONS, RIPLEY ENTERTAINMENT INC.

You hold in your hands an interactive book!

Fan the pages and watch the cool little people in the coaster car in the bottom right hand corner of each page!

Contributors

With a lot of help from my amusement park and ride fan friends, you are holding in your hands the most diverse compendium of the greatest fun facts, stories, trivia and oddities about the amusement industry that has ever been printed! When I first started this project, I put the call out and ended up with enough of these great little gems to put out several volumes of these books!

First of all, I'd like to thank Jim Futrell, an author in his own right, and probably the guy who knows more about this industry than anyone, for his eagle eye in helping fact check the Believe It or Not's in this book. Also, thanks to Disney's Marty Sklar for looking over the Disney chapter to make sure I did the mouse proud.

Several others stepped up to the loading platform with a bounty of fun facts. They included Mark Wyatt, Keith Miller, Paul Ruben, Carl Hughes, Alan Ramsay, Rick Davis, Mark Davidson, Jeffrey Siebert, Ron Gustafson, Cyndy Hanks, Marcus Gaines, and Kristiana Lemon.

Hoping that I haven't left anyone off, and apologizing if I did, here are the rest of the faithful group who took time to take a ride on this project: Gary Slade, Angela Fedders, Jiri Machalek, Crystal Kranz, Kristie Harreld, Arthur Levine, John Conway, Chester Tumidajewicz, Bryan L. Temmer, John Wood, Myra Woods, George LaCross, Mark Wijman, Nick Kondrat, Talley Green, David Bird, Tim Baldwin, Kathy Burrows, Ginny Davis, Brigid Fuller, Jeff Croushore, Adam Sandy, Rachel Lockitt, and Richard Harris.

Thanks to all, you are now a part of Ripley history!

Magical Midway

Originally a pleasure garden, Denmark's Bakken is the world's oldest operating amusement park – founded in 1583!

Lake Compounce is the oldest continuously operated amusement park in the United States – founded in 1846!

No Noise Thriller - If riders on the Scandia Screamer at the Scandia Family Fun Center scream during their thrill ride, they will not be permitted to ride again! Management encourages riders to cover their mouths if they think they might make a noise!

The beaches at New York's Coney Island were popular as early as the 1920s, but it was the completion of the area's first railroad in 1875 that helped make it the country's first mega-popular seaside resort.

Check index, starting on page 105 for location of parks and attractions featured throughout this book.

GUESTS AT THE DUTCH VILLAGE
HAVE THE OPPORTUNITY
TO STEP UPON
THE HEKSENWAAG —
AN AUTHENTIC 200-YEAR-OLD
WITCH SCALE THAT WILL DETERMINE,
BY WEIGHT, IF A PERSON *IS OR IS NOT*
A WITCH. IF ONE IS FOUND *NOT* GUILTY
OF WITCHCRAFT, THE PERSON WILL
RECEIVE A SIGNED AND DATED
"CERTIFICATE of INNOCENCE."

KENNETH WAITE
- famous clown -
WALKED
4602 MILES
WEARING HIS
CLOWN SHOES
3 FT. LONG!

Believe It or Not! Popular exhibits at Coney Island's Luna Park in 1903 and Massachusetts's Wonderland Park in 1906 were fully operating maternity wards, with premature babies on display in incubators.

Complete with private suites, the dog kennel at Dollywood is known as Doggywood.

New York's Playland Park opened in 1928 as the first major totally planned amusement park – serving as a prototype for today's highly designed theme parks!

At the Mall of America's Underwater Adventure Aquarium in Bloomington, Minn., people can pay $10 to name a Mackerel after their least favorite person and have it fed to a shark!

Captain Paul Boyton's Chutes Park, which opened in Chicago in 1894, was the first amusement park to charge an admission, using its rides and attractions as the main draw.

Six Flags Over Texas was the first theme park in the world to charge a pay-one-price admission - good for all rides, shows, and attractions inside the park.

Believe It or Not! More than 2,000 amusement parks were operating in the US in 1910.

During the 1920s, the Golden Age of Amusement Parks, nearly every mid to large American city and every resort area had at least one park of its own.

America's Great Depression, 1929-1933, ended the Golden Age of Amusement Parks, causing the collapse of more than 1,500 parks from coast to coast.

Gorilla My Dreams! "Koko," a gorilla at the Gorilla Foundation in Woodside, Calif., chose her mate by looking at videos of males from several other zoos!

A bellhop at Cedar Point's Hotel Breakers typically walks about 900 miles every season.

Believe It or Not! Former US President Richard Nixon once worked as a sideshow barker!

WHAT'S IN A NAME?

The Gillian family-owned waterpark in Ocean City, N.J. - **Gillian's Island.**

The citizens of Pen Argyl, Pa. were so proud of their new city-owned amusement park that they named it **Weona** (as in we own a) **Park!**

The waterpark at Lagoon Park - **Lagoona Beach.**

The largest waterpark in the Wisconsin Dells - **Noah's Ark!**

Lee Merrick named the little park he created in Marshall, Wis. - **Little A-Merrick-A.**

Billing itself as a "tropical island in the last frontier" is Alaska's largest indoor waterpark - **H2Oasis.**

A 20 foot long, 8-ton treadmill was built for Maggie the elephant at the Alaska Zoo after it was determined she needed to lose 1,000 pounds.

At the Denver (Colo.) Zoo, the orangutans receive daily aromatherapy treatments with oils extracted from Angelica Basil and Chamomile!

Kiddielands, a post war phenomenon during the early 1950s, were built to amuse the new crop of kids, known collectively today as the Baby Boomers. At one time, there were more than 200 of these parks in operation.

AIN'T HE PURDY?

WHAT WAS THOUGHT TO BE A WAX FIGURE OF A HANGED MAN IN A FUNHOUSE TURNED OUT TO BE **THE PRESERVED BODY** OF *ELMER McCURDY* WHO WAS KILLED IN A *1911 SHOOTOUT!* **W**ORKMEN AT THE PIKE AMUSEMENT PARK DISCOVERED THE TRUTH IN THE 1970'S WHEN THEY ATTEMPTED TO REATTACH AN ARM THAT HAD BROKEN OFF— *AND FOUND A BONE!*

More than 100 US parks closed their doors between 2000 and 2007, mostly due to land values that increased to the point that it wasn't viable to do anything but sell to developers. More than half of those have shut down since 2004.

During the late 1940s the lines at the Cordelia Knott's Chicken Dinner Restaurant were so long that she and her husband Walter felt they needed to create a diversion to keep the guests entertained and happy while waiting to get into the restaurant. The challenge of entertaining the growing crowds led Walter to create an authentic Old West Ghost Town adjacent to the restaurant. The attraction eventually grew into what is now Knott's Berry Farm Theme Park.

The 90-ton Dollywood Express coal-fired steam train offers passengers a 5 mile journey – the longest theme park train ride in North America!

The first Ripley's Believe It or Not! permanent museum with Robert Ripley's personal collection of the weird and unusual opened in St. Augustine, Fla., in December 1950, about a year after his death. The attraction still flourishes today!

Six Flags Over Texas opened on Aug. 1, 1961 - as America's first regional theme park.

Step Right Up! In 2006, 3.2 million Cedar Point guests played 3.65 million games - winning 600,000 prizes!

C.C. Macdonald and Charlie Presser designed and patented the Fishing Pond game at Idlewild in the early 1940s.

The first Skee-Ball tournament was held in an Atlantic City, N.J. arcade in 1932.

Nolan Bushnell, the father of the video game industry, envisioned the idea at an amusement park as he watched people throw baseballs at bottles.

Busy Buckets! Guests won 40,000 basketballs in 2006 at Carowinds - at only 3 basketball skill games!

Kennywood and New York's Playland Park are the only two US parks listed as National Historic Landmarks.

Thunder River white water rapids ride at AstroWorld was the first of its kind in the world. In 1980, park manager Bill Crandall imagined it while watching kayaks racing down a manmade river at the Olympics in Munich, Germany.

A Family Story

A young family walked onto the Christmas Plaza at Holiday World and stopped in front of the large, colorful statue of Santa. There stood Mom, Dad, and their four year old daughter looking up at the huge concrete icon.

The father pointed out the statue to his daughter, "Look, honey, there he is! You've been waiting and waiting to see him! Who is it?"

The little girl thought for a second and then her face broke into gleeful recognition. She let out a joyous squeal and ran toward the statue as fast as her chubby little legs could take her.

"MICKEY," the little girl proclaimed!

"JOHNNY WEISSMULLER," ONE OF THE FIRST MEN TO PORTRAY "TARZAN" IN THE MOVIES, SET THE WORLD 220-YARD FREESTYLE SWIMMING RECORD IN GEAUGA LAKE'S NEW OLYMPIC SIZE SWIMMING POOL!

Six Flags Over Texas, the original Six Flags park, was named for the six nations that have governed the state through the years: Spain, France, Mexico, the Republic of Texas, the Confederacy and the US.

The six flags that fly over Six Flags St. Louis are those of the US, Missouri, France, Illinois, Great Britain, and Spain.

SHAMU,
THE FIRST KILLER WHALE
TO SURVIVE IN CAPTIVITY,
WAS PURCHASED BY
SEA WORLD FOUNDER GEORGE MILLAY
IN 1965 FOR $35,000!

The six flags that give Six Flags Over Georgia its name belong to Georgia, Britain, Spain, France, the Confederacy, and the US.

Talk about air time! Silverwood theme park was an airstrip before being converted to a theme park.

Knoebels Amusement Resort utilizes rides and equipment from more than 50 different parks.

More than coasters! The world's largest breeding program for the endangered Asian Elephant is located at Busch Gardens Africa.

Two American theme parks have cave tours as part of their offerings – Onyx Cave at Guntown Mountain and Marvel Cave at Silver Dollar City.

The world's first log flume opened in 1963 at Six Flags Over Texas.

Great Views! The 125-acre Rocky Point Amusement Park property featured more than 1 1/2 miles of coastline with hills, fields, rocky cliffs, caves, beaches and forests.

It's Showtime! Based on averages, if you rode every ride in America's amusement parks and watched every show, you'd spend at least twice the amount of time watching than riding.

THE WORD FUN APPEARS IN MORE AMUSEMENT PARK NAMES THAN DOES ANY OTHER DESCRIPTIVE WORD!

The Miss California beauty pageant was created by Santa Cruz Beach Boardwalk founder Fred Swanton in 1924 to help attract visitors to Santa Cruz. However, much of the town was not appreciative and opposed the pageant because of the skimpy bathing suits the young ladies wore!

Virginia's Gift Shop at Knott's Berry Farm, which opened in the 1930s, is the oldest continuously operated theme park gift shop in the US.

ALIEN APEX RESORT,

THE FIRST EXCLUSIVE ALIEN/UFO THEME PARK IN THE UNITED STATES IS IN THE PLANNING STAGES AND WILL BE BASED ON THE PERFECT *UFO LOCATION* ON PLANET EARTH, NAMELY, *ROSWELL, NEW MEXICO,* THE SITE OF THE LEGENDARY *1947 UFO LANDING.*

Since 1988, Cedar Point has donated nearly $200,000 to local charities - all from its Loose Change Fund - money found underneath rides, along the midway and in the park's water features.

The Eiffel Tower exists, albeit one-third scale, in two American parks - Kings Island and Kings Dominion.

Local parks were built at the end of urban trolley tracks in the late 1880s by local trolley companies to help generate weekend business. The development of these popular parks, today known as Trolley Parks, created a new era of non-seaside amusement facilities in the US and at one time numbered in the hundreds.

Carowinds has the North Carolina – South Carolina state line running through the middle of the park. While a unique distinction, it creates its share of headaches, including different state-mandated break times, employment procedures, and state income tax rules.

Before closing for good at the end of the 2006 season, the owners of Erieview Park made their own wine in the park's Firehouse Winery. The park is now gone but the winery remains in business!

Dolly Parton is an owner of Dollywood, but her former singing buddy Kenny Rogers, doesn't own Kennywood Park, which is nearly 50 years older than the singer!

Six Flags Great Adventure has the largest drive-through safari outside Africa.

Robert Ripley once named the historic Idlewild train depot as the "smallest full service train depot in the United States." The 9 foot by 16 foot building was built in 1878 and still sits in its original spot, now on a midway in the park that follows the path of the original train tracks.

The 7-acre, Nickelodeon-themed park (formerly Knott's Camp Snoopy), in the middle of the Mall of America, Bloomington, Minn., is located on the site of the Old Metropolitan Stadium. There's a brass replica of the stadium's home plate, exactly where it sat, on one of the pathways of the indoor park.

ICONIC PIONEERS FROM OHIO INCLUDE NEAL ARMSTRONG, THE FIRST MAN ON THE MOON; THE WRIGHT BROTHERS, CREATORS OF THE FIRST AIRPLANE; AND LA MARCUS ADNA THOMPSON WHO IS CREDITED FOR INVENTING THE ROLLER COASTER IN 1884.

MONUMENT TO THE MEMORY OF THE PASSENGER PIGEON
Wyalusing State Park, Wisc.
THE PASSENGER PIGEON – NOW EXTINCT – ONCE DARKENED THE SKIES BY
THE BILLIONS – A FLOCK SOMETIMES REQUIRED A WEEK TO FLY PAST
The Last Bird Died in the Cincinnati Zoo in 1914

In late 1996, Gena Romano, the former owner of Brooklyn's Nellie Bly Park, became the first female president of the International Assn. of Amusement Parks & Attractions, the largest amusement park trade group in the world.

A stroll past all the trade show exhibits at the annual convention of the International Assn. of Amusement Parks & Attractions is a long walk - more than 7 miles!

A *Los Angeles Times* reporter visiting Magic Mountain on opening day in 1971 fell and broke his leg when the funicular on which he was riding came to a jolting stop. The reporter later wrote - "The owners call it Magic Mountain, but it should be called Tragic Mountain."

It took Holiday World, which opened as Santa Claus Land on Aug. 3, 1946, 50 seasons to top 500,000 in attendance and only eight additional years to top one million, which it did for the first time during the 2006 season.

There are 225 miles of utility piping installed under Universal's Islands of Adventure – enough for 2,300 homes!

In 1930, there were more than 1,000 miniature golf courses - in New York City!

The Name Tells it All!

Twisted Sisters - Original name of the Twisted Twins racing wooden coasters at Six Flags Kentucky Kingdom.

Serial Thriller - Inverted coaster at the now defunct Six Flags AstroWorld. Original name for the inverted coaster now known as the Thunderhawk at Geauga Lake.

Deju Vu - Boomerang coasters at Six Flags Great America, Six Flags Magic Mountain and Six Flags Over Georgia.

Fairly Odd Coaster - Junior woodies at Kings Island and Carowinds.

Fred - Unofficial name of log flume at Knoebels Amusement Resort.

Gravity Defying Corkscrew - Corkscrew coaster moved to Silverwood from Knott's Berry Farm, where it had debuted as the first-ever corkscrew.

Great White - Steel coaster at SeaWorld Texas - built in 1997 as the first roller coaster at any US SeaWorld park.

Gully Washer - Rapids ride at Six Flags Fiesta Texas.

Hangman - Inverted coaster at Wild Adventures and the now defunct Opryland Theme Park.

Skloosh - Log flume at Knoebels Amusement Resort.

Mind Eraser - Inverted coasters at Six Flags America and Six Flags New England.

Oki Doki - Junior steel coaster at Bobbejaanland, Lichtaart, Belgium.

Poison Ivy's Tangled Train - Steel family coaster at Six Flags New England.

Vertical Velocity - Impulse coaster at Six Flags Great America; V2: Vertical Velocity is the impulse coaster at Six Flags Discovery Kingdom (formerly Six Flags Marine World).

Sooperdooperlooper - Single looping coaster at Hersheypark since 1977.

Steel Eel - Steel coaster at SeaWorld Texas.

Texas Chute Out - Parachute drop at Six Flags Over Texas.

Up-'n'-Atom - Steel coaster at the now defunct Rocky Point Park.

Wallis's Wonderful Wriggling Wirral Wacky Worm - Steel coaster at England's Wallis' Family Fun Fair.

Whoopee Baby Scenic - Wooden coaster at the now defunct Neptune Beach, Alameda, Calif., 1927.

X:\ No Way Out - Steel coaster at Thorpe Park, Chertsey, Surrey, UK.

HERE BUNNY BUNNY!
CONEY ISLAND OF NEW YORK CITY
WAS NAMED AFTER THE RABBIT, OR *CONEY*,
BECAUSE OF THE UNUSUALLY LARGE POPULATION
OF THE FURRY LITTLE GUYS LIVING THERE.

In November 1993, the famous Ripley's Believe It or Not! comic strip featured a 4 foot, 10 inch tall daffodil that Geoffrey Thompson of Blackpool (England) Pleasure Beach grew in his English garden.

SOFT LANDING!
AVIATION GREAT
GLENN H. CURTISS
ESTABLISHED A WORLD RECORD
FOR FLYING OVER WATER WHEN
HE COMPLETED A 65-MILE LONG
FLIGHT FROM EUCLID BEACH TO THE
CEDAR POINT BEACH IN 1910.

Virginians Against America! Marriott's Great America (1976) and Disney's America (1994), two patriotic and historical themed parks proposed for the Manassas, Va. area, both failed to get local approval to be built.

Fungus Forces Out Santa!

Finland's popular Santa Park is the only theme park within the Arctic Circle, but its location inside a manmade mountain cavern in Lapland has caused a unique problem. In spring 2007, the subterranean attraction became the first park ever to be forced to close down its entire facility - due to a fungus and mildew outbreak! Santa was relocated for the summer months while the park was being scrubbed down, preparing for a fall reopening.

Two genres of theme parks – the themed marine park (SeaWorld) and the waterpark (Wet'n Wild) – were the creation of one pioneering genius - George Millay.

Galaxyland, which opened as Fantasyland on March 15, 1986 inside the West Edmonton Mall, Edmonton Alberta, Can., is the world's largest indoor theme park, complete with a triple-looping coaster, The Mindbender.

Theme Park Religion! Dollywood's full time chaplain leads all-denominational services in the park's historic chapel each Sunday morning from April through October and candlelight services every Sunday evening during November and December.

SANTA'S LAP

IS AVAILABLE ALL SUMMER LONG AT **7** NORTH AMERICAN THEME PARKS —

HOLIDAY WORLD, SANTA CLAUS, Ind.
SANTA'S LAND, CHEROKEE, N.C.
SANTA'S LAND, PUTNEY, Vt.
SANTA'S VILLAGE, JEFFERSON, N.H.
SANTA'S VILLAGE, BRACEBRIDGE, Ont., CANADA
SANTA'S WORKSHOP, NORTH POLE, Colo.
AND SANTA'S WORKSHOP, NORTH POLE, N.Y.

DURING ITS 100 YEARS IN BUSINESS,
NATIONAL TICKET COMPANY
HAS PRINTED AND SOLD
NEARLY **200 BILLION TICKETS**!

Almost condos! Wishing to preserve the second oldest amusement park in the country, the historic 1898 Midway Park, the state of New York bought it in October 2006 - for $4 million.

During its colorful history, New Jersey's Great Adventure has been owned by a gaming company (Bally's), a railroad (Penn Central), and a communications company (Time-Warner).

Nearly 1,000 teeth are broken off the dinosaur models each year by guests at the three DinoParks in Central Europe.

27

THE BETTY BOOP STORE,

FEATURING EVERYTHING *BETTY BOOP,* AT UNIVERSAL'S ISLANDS OF ADVENTURE IS THE *LARGEST* GIFT SHOP IN THE WORLD DEDICATED *TO THE BOOP-OOP-A-DOOP GIRL.*

The Miniland USA section of Legoland California features nearly 1,400 bonsai trees!

Colored vinyl tubes are used at Schlitterbahn East waterpark - chlorinated water causes black tubes to make marks on the pool walls.

When the US Congress declared war on Japan in 1941, the American manufacturing landscape was transformed with most factories converting their machinery to wartime use. At the Spillman Engineering Company, a major carousel manufacturer in North Tonawanda, N.Y., hands that previously turned out merry-go-rounds abandoned their wood-carving talents to machine landing gear housings for the P-39 Bell Airacobra, one of the US Army's swiftest and deadliest pursuit fighters.

If one steps upon Hiram McTavish's grave in the Boot Hill cemetery at Knott's Berry Farm, the beat of his heart can still be felt – decades after his death!

Celebrating its 100th anniversary in 2007, Hersheypark was originally created by Milton S. Hershey as a recreational area for his chocolate factory workers and their families.

A tongue-in-cheek park fan organization: National Enthusiasts of Rollercoasters and Darkrides – is known as NERD!

Dutch Village is the only North American theme park in which wooden shoes are carved.

OTIS T. CARR
BUILT THE

OTC X-1

FLYING SAUCER AMUSEMENT RIDE
AT FRONTIER CITY IN 1959
TO DEMONSTRATE HOW HIS **REAL** FLYING SAUCER
WOULD TRANSPORT HIM TO THE **MOON!**
THE FLIGHT NEVER HAPPENED AND THE
ONLY TRIP CARR MADE **WAS TO JAIL** —
FOR DEFRAUDING INVESTORS IN THE PROJECT.

Robert Ripley opened his first attraction, Ripley's Believe It or Not! Odditorium, at the 1933 Chicago World's Fair and the acts and exhibits were so intense that visitors kept fainting - requiring that doctors and nurses be on duty during operating hours.

Santa's Village in Bracebridge, Ont. Canada is located on the 45th parallel – exactly half way to the North Pole from the equator.

Wanting to extend the tourist season at his hotel in 1994, Stan Anderson, owner of the Polynesian Resort in the Wisconsin Dells, took waterpark equipment inside to his pool and in the process - is cited for starting the indoor waterpark resort phenomenon.

Where Are You? The Memphis Kiddie Park, founded in 1952, is located in Brooklyn, Ohio, a Cleveland suburb.

P.T. BARNUM

FAMOUS CIRCUS MAN
WHO SAID : -
" THERE'S A SUCKER
BORN EVERY MINUTE "
— WAS *HIMSELF* THE MOST GULLIBLE OF MEN

BARNUM WAS SWINDLED ON SUCH
RIDICULOUS SCHEMES AS
" ARTIFICIAL SNOW "
" BEAR GREASE "
" CHERRY-COLORED
CAT " ETC.

Ripley Classic 1931

BELIEVE IT OR NOT!...

RIPLEY ENTERTAINMENT INC.

GRAZ

IS THE
WORLD'S LARGEST OPERATOR
OF SMALL ATTRACTIONS —
WITH MORE THAN 60 IN 11 COUNTRIES!
INCLUDING —
☆ BELIEVE IT OR NOT! ODDITORIUMS,
☆ GUINNESS WORLD RECORD MUSEUMS,
☆ LOUIS TUSSAUD'S WAX WORKS,
☆ RIPLEY'S HAUNTED ADVENTURES,
☆ RIPLEY'S MOVING THEATRES 4-D,
☆ RIPLEY'S MINI GOLF
☆ ST. AUGUSTINE SIGHTSEEING TRAINS,
AND RIPLEY'S AQUARIUMS!
IT ALSO OWNS THE —
GREAT WOLF LODGE
NIAGARA FALLS, CANADA,
WHICH INCLUDES A 103,000 SQUARE FOOT
INDOOR WATERPARK!

Harold Chance, the pioneering ride manufacturer who founded Chance Rides, is the only person who has been inducted into three major industry halls of fame: International Assn. of Amusement Parks & Attractions, 1991; the Outdoor Amusement Business Assn., 2003; and the Showman's League of America, 2005.

The Castle of Terror, a Bill Tracy designed dark ride, debuted in 1963 at Rocky Point Park and was known for its horrific dioramas. When the Castle first opened, the park billed the experience as being so terrifying that management needed to station a nurse at the unloading area in case riders needed medical attention. Female park employees took shifts donning the nurse costume. The novelty wore off after the ride's first month of operation and the "nurses" were redeployed back to operating rides and games. It is not known whether or not a nurse was ever pressed into service.

The lighthouse at the entrance to Universal's Islands of Adventure is modeled after the ancient lighthouse of Pharos in Alexandria, Egypt.

It's Ride Time! Cedar Point provides thrills to nearly 241,000 riders a day and to more than 35 million every season! On average, each guest enjoys 11 rides during their daily visit.

The most picked up piece of litter at any amusement park in the world - cigarette butts.

Cheap Rides! All 16 rides at Bay Beach Amusement Park cost 50-cents or less!

Cod liver oil, which supposedly makes people strong and healthy, is offered free to guests at Kongeparken in Norway. Those who sample it receive a token for a game that is fixed to show their immediate improved strength!

Cincinnati's Coney Island, the 15th oldest park in North America, is home to Sunlite Pool, the world's largest recirculating swimming pool. It is 200 feet by 401 feet, holds 3 million gallons of water and has 6 diving boards!

Dollywood was known as Goldrush Junction during the 1970s and was owned by the Cleveland Browns football team.

The first wave pool in America was built in 1970 at Point Mallard Park in Decatur, Ala.

TIVOLI SPELLED BACKWARD IS "I LOV IT"

Putt around the Province! The miniature golf course at Upper Clements (NS) Theme Park is on a Nova Scotia shaped island in a lake in the middle of the park.

The Wall Street Journal called Amphibiville, a 2-acre wetland exhibit at the Detroit Zoo the "Disneyland for toads."

THE ICONIC KILLER WHALE OF SEA WORLD FAME, HAS HIS OWN (UNOFFICIAL) WEB PAGE ON MYSPACE·COM.

While serving at Fort Ligonier during the French and Indian War, George Washington heard of a conflict between the French and British forces, less than three miles away. Washington led a group of volunteers from the post to help out, but in the darkness, the British troop's leader, Lieutenant Colonel Mercer and his men mistook the volunteers as the enemy and killed 14 of the men. Washington rushed between the opposing commands, pushing up rifles to prevent further unnecessary bloodshed. He later recalled that he had never been in greater danger than in those moments between the firing lines. Though the exact location of that battle has not been determined, it is widely believed to have taken place at what is now Idlewild Park.

Colo, a Western Lowland Gorilla, the world's first to be born in captivity in 1956, still lives at the Columbus (Ohio) Zoo. Her family tree includes 3 children, 16 grandchildren and 4 great grandchildren.

Bright Idea! Each year, Busch Gardens Europe and the adjacent Water Country USA recycle 1.5 tons of old light bulbs.

A series of 1930s Believe It or Not! cartoons mentioning Santa Claus, Ind. lead to great interest in the town and soon several commercial developments were launched, including Santa Claus Land on Aug. 3, 1946, by Louis J. Koch, which many consider the world's first theme park. Today, the park is known as Holiday World and is run by Koch's grandson, Will Koch.

Squeak, Squeak! More than 500 cans of WD-40 are used each year at Hersheypark!

Carowinds safely provided more than 13,350,000 rides in 2006.

"ALFUNDO"
THE DECADES-LONG MASCOT FOR DORNEY PARK IN ALLENTOWN, Pa., WAS SO NAMED BECAUSE "AL-LENTOWN HAS FUN AT DO-RNEY."

Dance, Putt & Roll! The historic dance pavilion at Quassy Amusement Park has had many lives since opening in 1915 as an open-air dance hall. In 1939 it was converted into a roller rink. In 1964, miniature golf replaced skating and in 1969 electric bumper cars replaced golf. In 1972 the building was transformed into a games arcade, which it remains today!

Jones's Woods, a 153-acre entertainment mecca on Manhattan Island, NY, just 15 miles from Coney Island, is widely accepted as the first large US amusement resort. Beer drinking and dancing in the beer gardens were its most popular activities!

Scientist Samual Botsford conducted a series of unsuccessful experiments in electricity on Lake Compounce in October 1846. However, thanks to the large crowds and major publicity garnered by the experiments, the lake's owner Gad Norton was able to quickly develop the land into a picturesque picnic park. Today the park is the oldest continuously operated amusement park in America.

Nearly 150 million people visit the 200-plus facilities accredited by the AZA (Association of Zoos & Aquariums) each year – less than 122 million voted in the last US presidential election!

Approximately 330 million visits were registered at US amusement and theme parks in 2006, more than those attending every professional baseball, football and basketball game – combined!

What a Ride! The American Police Hall of Fame and Museum in Titusville, Fla. sells rides in a high-speed police helicopter – for $22!

Two of Santa Cruz Beach Boardwalk's classic rides - the Looff Carousel and the Giant Dipper were built by father and son. Charles I.D. Looff built the hand-carved merry-go-round in 1911, his son Arthur Looff built the wooden coaster in 1924.

The Great Pasha was buried alive for two hours for a stunt at Ideal Beach (now Indiana Beach) on July 13, 1930 - and survived! Publicity stated: "He will be placed in the coffin in the dance garden. Tickets are 10-cents and will be good for burial and resurrection in front of the grand stand." Local funeral directors placed Pasha in the coffin and helped bury him alive!

The first professional competition on a man-made wave took place at Schlitterbahn in 1992 on the Boogie Bahn surf ride.

President Rutherford B. Hayes was the first US president to use a telephone! While visiting Rocky Point Park on June 28, 1877, the president talked with Alexander Graham Bell who was at a hotel, 12 miles away!

Lake Winnepesaukah is a Native American word meaning "bountiful waters" or "beautiful lake of the highlands." Members of the Cherokee nation inhabited the property that is now the amusement park and used the spring fed lake to operate a grist mill.

Ocean Breeze Waterpark has a 45 foot tall gorilla mascot - Hugh Mongous!

"ANIMALS ALWAYS"
AT THE ST. LOUIS ZOO
IS THE LARGEST SCULPTURE
AT **ANY** PUBLIC ZOO IN THE U.S.
IT IS **36-FEET TALL, 130-FEET LONG**
AND WEIGHS **100 TONS!**

Construction on a Noah's Ark funhouse in 1936 at Kennywood Park was delayed several times – due to heavy rains and severe flooding!

One of a kind! Once a staple of the amusement park and carnival industries of the early 1950s, there is only one Allan Herschell Looper left operating at a park in the US today – at Knoebels Amusement Resort.

41

MARINELAND of FLORIDA,
THE WORLD'S FIRST OCEANARIUM FOUNDED IN 1938 AS A MOVIE STUDIO, IS LOCATED IN THE TOWN OF MARINELAND, Fla., WHICH HAS A GREATER DOLPHIN POPULATION THAN HUMAN!

To protest "high taxes on living," Paul Abbot spent 10 weeks at the bottom of Lake Shafer at Ideal Beach (now Indiana Beach) in a 10 foot by 6 foot by 6 foot tank in 1950. Worldwide publicity drew thousands to the park to witness the stunt. Park owner Tom Spackman won the industry's "outstanding promotion of the year" award from the national parks association for the event.

Al Capone's "career" started in a saloon on Coney Island, NY.

Hollywood film stars were told by their studios to stay away from miniature golf courses in 1930! They didn't want it to appear that the stars were endorsing the popular sport that had cut into film attendance by 25% that year alone!

Workers cleaning out a small lake at the Blackpool (England) Pleasure Beach in 2006 found a gold and pearl earring that once belonged to Hollywood actress Marlene Dietrich. She had reported it lost following a ride on the park's Big Dipper roller coaster – in 1934!

Ripley Classic 1941

AL McKEE
DRIVER OF THE SCENIC RAILWAY
Palisades Amusement Park
TRAVELED 45,000 MILES WITHOUT
GOING ANYWHERE

PARK OWNER GEORGE C. TILYOU
OF STEEPLECHASE PARK ON CONEY ISLAND
CHARGED A 10-CENT ADMISSION
FOR PEOPLE TO TOUR "THE BURNING RUINS"
FOLLOWING A DEVASTATING FIRE
THAT DESTROYED MUCH OF THE PARK IN 1907.

Great at Puppets, Terrible at Parks!

Puppeteering brothers Sid and Marty Krofft were introduced to theme park entertainment in 1964 when Angus Wynne Jr. hired them to create puppet shows for his new park, Six Flags Over Texas. The brothers went out on their own in 1976 to create the $14 million World of Sid & Marty Krofft in the Omni International in Atlanta. The indoor park experienced the quickest demise of a major amusement facility in US history – lasting only 5 months, 17 days!

The main attraction at the World of Sid & Marty Krofft was The Pinball Machine, a life size custom-built amusement ride! Guests rode inside a 6-foot round pinball as they were shot through flippers and bumpers into holes with flashing lights.

Sharon Patrick, one of the seven original Sea Maids at SeaWorld San Diego in 1964, had great success after leaving Shamu and friends. In 1997 she became president of Martha Stewart Living Omnimedia, becoming its CEO in 2003!

The C.P. Huntington train is the most popular production model train ever developed. Chance Rides of Wichita has built more than 400 of them since selling the first one to Wichita's Joyland Amusement Park in 1961 where it is still in operating condition.

Coney Island, NY, has never been one major amusement park – it's a seaside area that has always featured a variety of independent concessionaires along with its full-size parks!

COLLEGE FOOTBALL LEGEND AND NOTRE DAME GREAT **KNUTE ROCKNE** WORKED AS A LIFEGUARD AT CEDAR POINT WITH TEAMMATE GUS DORAIS IN 1913. DURING THEIR FREE TIME, THEY PERFECTED **THE FORWARD PASS** ON THE CEDAR POINT BEACH.

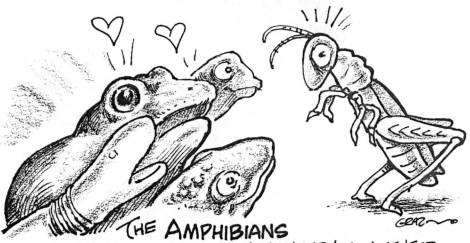

THE AMPHIBIANS
AT THE NATIONAL AMPHIBIAN CONSERVATION CENTER
AT THE DETROIT ZOO ARE A HUNGRY LOT.
THEY CONSUMED 6,214,000 CRICKETS
IN 2006!

By 1914, more than 1,000,000 revelers commonly visited Coney Island on a hot Sunday afternoon!

The Santa Claus World Congress is held each July at Bakken during which time more than 100 Santa's from around the world take classes on being Santa, while entertaining park guests!

Santa's Workshop, appropriately located in North Pole, NY, was among the first parks in the US to be built with a concise themed environment – 6 years before Disneyland opened!

Hot dog inventor Charles Feltman's grandson, Charles Feltman invented the "Mow-'Em-Down" shooting gallery during WWII, a few yards from his grandfather's famous restaurant. The game featured guns that players used to shoot pellets at German paratroopers.

Check index, starting on page 105 for location of parks and attractions featured throughout this book.

Roller Coasters

Lakemont Park's Leap the Dips, the last of the hundreds of Figure-8 style side friction coasters built in the U.S., was placed on the National Register of Historic Places in March 1991 and given National Landmark status in June 1996.

The Switchback Gravity Pleasure Railway, built by La Marcus A. Thompson at Coney Island in 1884 was the first true roller coaster in America. It took only three weeks for Thompson to recover the $1,600 it cost to build the ride.

Believe It or Not! 61-year old Richard Krieger made a 30-mile round trip bicycle journey from his home to Knott's Berry Farm three or four times a week to experience the Xcelerator roller coaster, which he rode 20,000 times between June 22, 2002 and Jan. 20, 2007!

Check index, starting on page 105 for location of parks and attractions featured throughout this book.

WHAT'S IN A NAME?

GRAZIAN

WHEN **CEDAR POINT** IN SANDUSKY, OHIO BUILT THE WORLD'S FASTEST AND LARGEST STEEL ROLLER COASTER IN 1989, THE PARK WANTED A POWERFUL NAME. IT CAME UP WITH **MAGNUM XL-200** — MAGNUM FOR POWERFUL, XL FOR **EXTRA LARGE** AND 200 FOR ITS HEIGHT.

One of the four Mir space stations built by the Russians is now a part of the theming at Europa-Park's $30 million Euro-Mir roller coaster.

Duck, Duck - DUCK! Model Fabio was a guest of Busch Gardens Williamsburg on March 20, 1999 for the media day preview of the park's new coaster, Apollo's Chariot. On the first ride of the day he was hit in the face − by a low flying goose!

During the 1920s, considered the Golden Age of Amusement Parks, there were more than 2,000 wooden roller coasters in the United States. In 2007 there were less than 150.

Only 120 roller coasters were built in the US between 1930 and 1972 − while 1,500 were destroyed!

More roller coasters opened worldwide in 2000 than in any other year, ever − 180!

The Timber Terror wooden roller coaster built in 1996 at Silverwood Theme Park was the first new woodie built in that state in 76 years.

Cedar Point's Magnum XL-200 opened in spring 1989 as the first of the hypercoaster genre of non-looping, over 200 foot tall steel roller coasters.

The Screamin' Eagle wooden roller coaster at Six Flags St. Louis was painted with Sears Weatherbeater paint and was featured in Sears' 1990s TV commercials.

So many skunks have been run over in the tunnel of the Blue Streak roller coaster at Conneaut Lake Park that many now refer to it as Skunk Tunnel.

NEVERMORE!

GRAZIANO

THE RAVEN AT HOLIDAY WORLD, SANTA CLAUS, IND., IS THE **ONLY** EDGAR ALLAN POE THEMED ROLLER COASTER *IN THE WORLD!*

Poe's *Raven* was first published in 1845. Holiday World's Raven premiered exactly 150 years later, in 1995.

Poe died mysteriously on Oct. 3, 1849. The final approval for naming The Raven Roller Coaster was given 145 years later...to the day!

The last sighting of ravens nesting in southern Indiana was in 1894, exactly 100 years before construction of The Raven Roller Coaster in Santa Claus, in southern Indiana.

Tim O'Brien, then with *Amusement Business* magazine, was the first to suggest the name Raven for what was to be the park's first wooden coaster. He is now with Ripley Entertainment and is the author of this edition of Believe It or Not!

AT THORPE PARK
IN SURREY, ENGLAND,
A RECORD
82 BRITISH
UNIVERSITY
STUDENTS
TOOK OFF
THEIR
CLOTHES
AND RODE
A ROLLER COASTER
NAKED!

Believe It or Not! There's enough lumber in the Texas Giant, the woodie at Six Flags Over Texas, to build 30 houses.

The first Corkscrew roller coaster, the first modern ride to successfully turn people upside down, opened on May 21, 1975 at Knott's Berry Farm at a cost of $700,000. It was relocated to Silverwood Theme Park in 1990 where it still operates.

The Great White opened at SeaWorld Texas in 1997 - the first roller coaster built at any SeaWorld theme park.

Extra sets of seat cushions were stored on the loading platform of the Flying Turns at Euclid Beach – to replace the wet ones soiled by frightened riders!

THE MANTIS ROLLER COASTER
AT CEDAR POINT
ORIGINALLY WAS GOING TO BE NAMED
BANSHEE —
UNTIL PARK MANAGEMENT DISCOVERED
THE DEFINITION OF BANSHEE INVOLVES
"A FEMALE SPIRIT WHOSE WAILING WARNS
OF AN IMPENDING DEATH."
NOT GOOD KARMA FOR A ROLLER COASTER!

Of the approximate 2,000 roller coasters in the world, only 20 of them are longer than a mile in length! Only four of them go faster than 100 mph.

The first looping wooden coaster was the Flip Flap, built in 1889 in Toledo, Ohio, by Linda Beecher!

Whish, Whoosh, What Was That? The Dueling Dragons racing steel inverted coasters at Universal's Islands of Adventures pass within 12 inches of each other three different times at speeds of up to 60 mph!

It took three years for land preparation, design and construction of The Beast wooden coaster at Kings Island.

The Runaway Mine Train built at Six Flags Over Texas in 1966 was the first $1 million ride built outside of a Disney park.

Blackpool (England) Pleasure Beach has more wooden roller coasters than any park anywhere else in the world – 5!

Believe It or Not! The Coney Island Thunderbolt coaster was built OVER the Kensington Hotel in 1925 which became the home of the coaster's owner Fred Moran. The final occupant, before the property was sold in 1988 was Mae Timpano. The house was featured in the movie *Annie Hall*.

Bat, the first suspended roller coaster, premiered at Kings Island in 1981, but was engineered so badly that it was scrapped after only two seasons.

With more than 70, California has at least 25 more roller coasters than does any other state.

The new Flying Turns at Knoebels Amusement Resort is the first of its genre of coaster built since the late 1930s and is the first to operate since the Flying Turns at Euclid Beach Park closed in 1969!

The Switchback Railway was the first of 30 roller coasters that would operate at Cedar Point through the years. It opened in 1892 with a 25 foot tall hill and a speed of 10 mph.

RIDERS ABOARD

THUNDER ROAD WOODEN RACING COASTERS AND THE **CAROLINA GOLDRUSHER** MINE TRAIN AT CAROWINDS, CROSS THE NORTH CAROLINA/ SOUTH CAROLINA BORDER *TWICE* DURING EACH RIDE!

Among the most extreme and frightening roller coasters of all times was the Revere Beach Lightning. During its second night of operation, a woman rider became hysterical and jumped to her death. The ride was closed for 20 minutes while the body was removed, during which time hundreds of people watched, some "notably impatient to ride!" During its turbulent six year history there were countless injuries to riders, including broken bones, fractured ribs and facial injuries. Eventually there were more people watching than riding and because the ride was no longer profitable, it was dismantled in 1933.

It took more than 600 miles of lumber to build the Son of Beast wooden roller coaster at Kings Island in 2000. Laid end to end, the wood would stretch from Cincinnati to New York City.

The first loop ever on a roller-coaster style ride was on the Centrifuge Railway at Frascati Gardens in Paris – in 1846!

The shape of the hills that cause "airtime" or the weightless sensation during a roller coaster ride is a parabolic curve, an exact mathematical shape discovered by Galileo during the 16th Century!

A roller coaster was featured in the background of a TV commercial – for Pepto-Bismol!

Elvis Presley's last public appearance was during an all night ride session in August 1977 on the Zippin Pippin wooden roller coaster at Libertyland in Memphis.

BATMAN THE RIDE

OPENED AT SIX FLAGS GREAT AMERICA
IN GURNEE, ILL. IN 1992
AS THE WORLD'S FIRST *INVERTED* ROLLER COASTER,
A RIDE ON WHICH RIDERS SIT BENEATH THE TRACK
WITH THEIR FEET DANGLING BENEATH THEM IN
THE OPEN AIR!

During its heyday, the legendary Cyclone at Crystal Beach was so intense that 5% who rode it passed out, requiring that a nurse be on duty at the station.

Ron Toomer is credited with the basic design of 80 coasters!

Believe It or Not! The first roller coaster that legendary coaster designer Ron Toomer ever rode was the very first roller coaster he ever designed in 1966 - the Runaway Mine Train at Six Flags Over Texas! He rode it once again - during the ride's 40th anniversary celebration!

The 310 foot tall Millennium Force and 420 foot tall Top Thrill Dragster, both coasters at Cedar Point, are taller than the Statue of Liberty.

Worldwide in 2007, 98 roller coasters had Dragon as part of their name; another 36 had Big as part of its moniker and another 18 had Cyclone as part of its title. That's all in addition to the 70 roller coasters that appropriately had Roller Coaster as part of their name!

Cedar Point has the most roller coasters of any park on this planet – 17!

More wooden roller coasters opened in 2000 than in any other year in modern coaster history (post-1955) - 15.

The highest capacity roller coaster in the world is Dueling Dragons at Universal's Islands of Adventure – 3,200 per hour!

The Mauch Chunk Switchback Railway in Jim Thorpe, Pa., built in 1827 to haul coal down from the mountains, was turned into a 9-mile long gravity amusement ride in the 1870s and within a few years, was the second most popular tourist attraction in the US, second only to Niagara Falls!

Pennsylvania has the most wooden coasters of any U.S. state – 17!

If all eight of Magic Mountain's looping coasters are ridden, the rider will be inverted 39 times - no other amusement park in the world will flip you more!

DOG DAZE!

CANNON BALL
THE CANINE,
LIVED UNDER *CANNON BALL*, THE COASTER
AT LAKE WINNEPESAUKAH FOR SEVEN YEARS
AND WOULD CHASE AFTER THE COASTER TRAIN
EVERY TIME IT LEFT THE STATION —
APPROX. 326,592 LAPS!

16 people have met and married as a result of joining the Roller Coaster Club of Great Britain. A higher success rate than the long running British dating show Blind Date!

Weekend Warriors! Mark and Missy Wyatt, Colleen Whyte, Bob Brodish, Ed Evans and Fred Wagaman traveled 1,239 miles on one weekend, June 3-5, 1988 and rode every operating roller coaster in Pennsylvania – 27 coasters in 16 parks!

The first roller coaster to top 100 mph – the Tower of Terror at Australia's Dreamland, opened in spring 1997, 51 days before Superman The Escape opened at California's Six Flags Magic Mountain – that also hit that magic speed.

Two wooden coasters are named after rattlesnakes – The Rattler at Six Flags Fiesta Texas, and the New Mexico Rattler at Cliff's Amusement Park.

The Hundeprut coaster, loosely translated as the dog fart coaster, at BonBon Land in Denmark, features a figure of a dog sitting in the middle of the ride with its tail raised and a pile of poop beneath it. The attraction has a tunnel in which riders hear the unmistakable sounds - of a dog farting!

Leap the Dips, a side friction wooden roller coaster at Lakemont Park was built in 1902, rebuilt in 1999, and is now the world's oldest operating roller coaster.

Check index, starting on page 105 for location of parks and attractions featured throughout this book.

Entertainers

The roller coasters of the now defunct Pike Amusement Park were featured in more than 20 movies, including *Abbott and Costello in Hollywood* (1945), *Gorilla at Large* (1954), and *It's Alive 3: Island of the Alive* (1987).

The rock group Boston was playing the midway stage at Rocky Point Park in summer 1975 when "discovered."

The best rock & roll amusement park lyrics ever written: "You'll never know how great a kiss can feel, when you're stuck at the top of a Ferris Wheel, when I fell in love....down at Palisades Park," were recorded by Freddy "Boom Boom" Cannon and penned by Chuck "Gong Show" Barris. Originally titled Amusement Park, it was changed to salute the now defunct popular park, across from Manhattan on New Jersey's palisades.

Freddy Cannon re-released the "Palisades Park" song as "Kennywood Park" in 1987, as a fund raiser for the Children's Hospital of Pittsburgh.

CROONER
PERRY COMO
WAS "DISCOVERED"
WHILE CUTTING HAIR AT THE
CONNEAUT LAKE HOTEL AT
CONNEAUT LAKE PARK, PA.

Teen idols of the 1980s, the New Kids on the Block, filmed their first music video at Deno's Wonder Wheel park in Coney Island.

The Everly Brothers broke up as a duo during a performance at Knott's Berry Farm on July 14, 1973. Phil smashed his guitar and walked off the stage to protest his brother Don's lackluster performance.

ACTOR **BRUCE WILLIS** WORKED FOR TWO SEASONS ON MOREY'S PIER IN WILDWOOD, N.J. AS AN AGE AND WEIGHT GUESSER!

Ripley Classic 1945

Ripley
5-15

EMMETT KELLY

WAS RINGLING BROS! **SAD** CLOWN FOR 15 YEARS.
AFTER LEAVING THE CIRCUS, HE BECAME THE
VP OF FUN AT PACIFIC OCEAN PARK, WHERE HIS
MAIN JOB WAS GREETING GUESTS!

SEA WOOF!

GRAZIANO

DURING THE SUMMER OF 1981 AT MARINELAND, FLORIDA, CANINE STAR **BENJI** BECAME THE FIRST DOG EVER TO **SCUBA DIVE!** HIS CUSTOM DIVING SUIT COST OVER **$10,000.**

Six Flags Magic Mountain, located 60 miles from Hollywood, is utilized often by movie and TV producers. Among its starring roles: the fictional park Walley World in 1983's *National Lampoon's Vacation;* as the background each week in the opening credits to the TV sitcom *Step by Step;* as the fictional park shown in *Encino Man;* played a major role in the 1977 film *Rollercoaster;* served as the roller coaster park in *Space Cowboys;* and was the backdrop of the TV movie *KISS Meets the Phantom of the Park.*

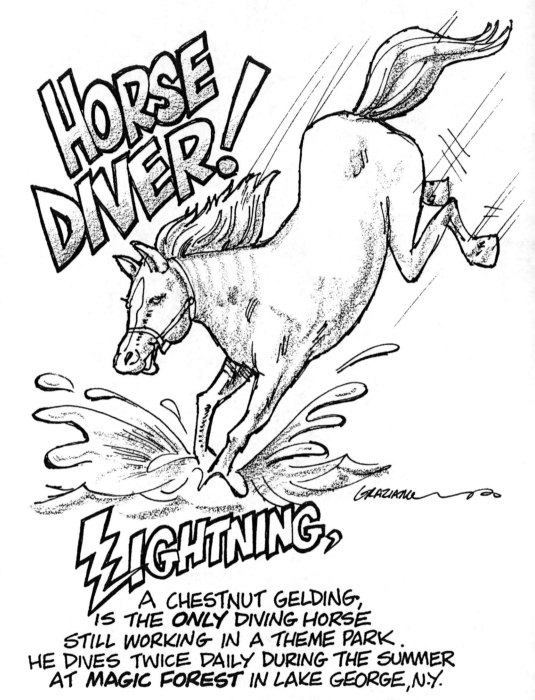

HORSE DIVER!

LIGHTNING, A CHESTNUT GELDING, IS THE **ONLY** DIVING HORSE STILL WORKING IN A THEME PARK. HE DIVES TWICE DAILY DURING THE SUMMER AT **MAGIC FOREST** IN LAKE GEORGE, N.Y.

Singer John Denver wanted to be a musician for Six Flags Over Texas, but park officials said he wasn't good enough – and turned him down!

The rock group Cars shot their first music video at Whalom Park.

What a blast! Oceanview Amusement Park closed down in 1978, but went out with a bang! It was featured in a 1979 TV disaster movie, "Death Of Oceanview Park," and was blown up as part of the plot.

As a tribute to their huge fan base in Salt Lake City in 1965, The Beach Boys wrote and recorded, "Salt Lake City," that spoke of Lagoon Park and noted that the city had the "cutest girls in the Western States." The Downtown Merchants Assn. was so impressed with the recording that they had 1,000 copies of the record pressed to use as a giveaway to help promote the city.

Cinesphere at Ontario Place in Toronto, Can., opened in 1971 as the first permanent IMAX® film theatre in the world. It is still in use!

In May 1965, the Beach Boys recorded "Amusement Parks USA," a little ditty that paid homage to several popular amusement parks of the time, including Riverview Park, Palisades Park, Pacific Ocean Park, Steel Pier, and Euclid Beach. The song didn't chart anywhere but Japan, where it reached Number 3!

AAYYYOOOHH!

One of the first people to ride Knott's Berry Farm's Timber Mountain Log Ride on its inaugural day, July 11, 1969, was JOHN WAYNE!

SeaWorld's star killer whale, Shamu, appeared in several movies, including *Dr. Doolittle 2* and *Jaws 3*.

A crowd of 8,488 crowded the new Paladium outdoor amphitheater at Carowinds on opening night, May 24, 1975 to watch country stars Jerry Reed and Dottie West.

Theme park fun for $600, Alex! Alex Trebek, host of the popular TV show Jeopardy read the answer "Holiday World is a theme park in this Indiana town that gets a lot of mail at Christmastime." The question was "What is Santa Claus, Alex?"

Check index, starting on page 105 for location of parks and attractions featured throughout this book.

Disney

Walt Disney World in Central Florida is 47-square miles in size, about twice the size of Manhattan Island in New York City.

The world's first tubular steel roller coaster - The Matterhorn - opened at Disneyland in 1959 and forever changed the face of roller coaster development.

The Magic Kingdom at Walt Disney World, built in 1971, cost $250 million - the most money spent to date to build a park anywhere in the world.

Walt Disney lived long enough to personally walk through only one of the parks named after him – California's Disneyland!

Disneyland's PeopleMover was built by Disney's Community Transportation division as a prototype. They built the second one for the Houston International Airport.

MARTY SKLAR, A WALT DISNEY *IMAGINEER* FOR MORE THAN **50 YEARS,** IS THE ONLY DISNEY EMPLOYEE WHO HAS ATTENDED THE OPENING OF *AND* HAS CONTRIBUTED TO ALL *11* OF DISNEY'S *MAJOR THEME PARKS!*

The popular It's a Small World ride was originally created by Walt Disney for the 1964 New York World's Fair and was moved to Disneyland and opened there on May 28, 1966. Small World rides then opened at Walt Disney World in Florida on Oct. 2, 1971; Tokyo Disneyland on April 15, 1983; and Disneyland Paris on April 12, 1992. It is set to open at Hong Kong Disneyland in 2008.

Funkiest Tree in Florida! The Tree of Life, the huge icon of Disney's Animal Kingdom, stands 145 feet tall, with a leafy canopy 160 feet across. Its trunk is 50 feet wide at the base, and it has a sprawling root base of 170 feet in diameter. The hand carved tree is a tapestry of more than 325 animals. There are 103,000 leaves glued to the tree's branches and it took a crew of more than a thousand workers 18 months to create. AND, there's a 4-D movie theater inside!

Each car on Epcot's Test Track ride was designed to travel one million miles, equivalent to four round trips to the moon!

The most 'populated' attraction at Disneyland Paris is It's a Small World. There are 281 Audio-Animatronic figures, 48 animated toys and 247 other animated items.

The storyline for Spaceship Earth at Epcot at Walt Disney World was developed by science fiction writer Ray Bradbury!

Opened in 1998, Disney's Animal Kingdom is the largest theme park Disney has ever built. Florida's Magic Kingdom, Epcot and Disney-MGM Studios parks all COMBINED would fit into the 580 acre Disney's Animal Kingdom, with room to spare.

Horticulturists at the Land pavilion in Walt Disney World's Epcot grow cucumbers, watermelons and pumpkins – in the shape of Mickey Mouse!

The car-themed Autopia attraction at Hong Kong Disneyland is the first Disney park to offer an all-electric version of this classic Disney ride!

Feng Shui masters were utilized during the planning stages of Hong Kong Disneyland and as a result, all entrances to the park, its attractions and public spaces were oriented to maximize good energy flow and to promote good fortune and well-being for Disney guests and cast members.

When US President Harry Truman, a Democrat, visited Disneyland, he refused to ride the Dumbo Flying Elephants because the animal was the symbol of the Republican Party!

"Heigh-ho! Heigh-ho! It's home from work we go!"

With approximately 50,000 "cast members," Walt Disney World is the largest single-site employer in the U.S.

Employees in the Magic Kingdom at Walt Disney World walk to their workstations via a series of underground tunnels. That's why you never see a person wearing a Tomorrowland uniform, for example, in Adventureland.

At Disney hotels worldwide, porters and bellhops are called Luggage Hosts.

There are more than 200 certified sommeliers working at Walt Disney World - more than any single company in the world!

Preserving the magic! When a guest vomits at a Disney park, a "protein spill" alert goes out to the custodial staff!

Epcot stands for Experimental Prototype Community of Tomorrow, not Every Paycheck Comes on Thursdays, as some Disney cast members claim!

DISNEYLAND,
AMERICA'S FIRST TRUE THEME PARK
OPENED AT 2:30 PM ON JULY 17, 1955
IN ANAHEIM, CALIF.,
AT A COST OF $17 MILLION!

The first general admission ticket sold for Disneyland in 1955 was purchased by Walt's brother, Roy - for $1.

Animal manure ranks third among recycled commodities for The Walt Disney Company, totaling more than 8,000 tons each year.

THE HARMONY

BARBER SHOP,
LOCATED IN
WALT DISNEY WORLD'S MAGIC KINGDOM,
SPECIALIZES IN *FIRST HAIRCUTS.*
DURING THE CUT, YOUNGSTERS RECEIVE
SPRINKLES OF PIXIE DUST, A CERTIFICATE
AND A SET OF MOUSE EARS —
ALL FOR $14!

Believe It or Not! The first guest in queue each morning for the Maelstrom ride at the Norway pavilion in Epcot receives a free Viking hat that reads, "Viking of the Day!"

Walt Disney originally envisioned a dome covering the "downtown" portion of the Epcot community in order to have complete control over the weather.

The idea for Disney-MGM Studios came from an idea to have a movie pavilion at Epcot. Once Imagineers realized that the range of possibilities using that theme were larger than just one attraction, the idea for a third theme park at Walt Disney World was born.

The Mickey Mouse ears that rest atop the Earfull Tower, the icon of Disney-MGM Studios, are size 342 3/8.

Mickey Mouse Park was the name originally proposed for Disneyland!

More than 4 million trees, plants, shrubs, ground-covers, vines, epiphytes and grasses from every continent on Earth - except Antarctica – representing 4,000 species, are growing at Disney's Animal Kingdom.

In the final bidding war, Disney chose France as its location to build the Euro Disney Resort project. Spain came in second.

There are 22 company-owned resorts in Disney World, with 24,000 rooms - more than most cities!

11-year old future film mogul George Lucas was among opening day guests at Disneyland in July 1955.

Believe It or Not! If a Mickey Mouse balloon pops while in a Disney park, it will be replaced free of charge!

The Osmond Brothers made their public singing debut at Disneyland in 1961 in the Carnation Gardens.

Both Disneyland in California and the Magic Kingdom at Walt Disney World in Florida are located in Orange County.

Tokyo Disneyland opened on April 15, 1983, The Walt Disney Company's first park venture outside North America.

Featuring more than 1,700 shows a day, Walt Disney World is the largest producer of live entertainment on a daily basis in the world.

AT NEARLY 200 FEET TALL, **EXPEDITION EVEREST** AT *DISNEY'S ANIMAL KINGDOM* IS THE *TALLEST* OF *18 MOUNTAINS* CREATED BY DISNEY IMAGINEERS AT DISNEY PARKS WORLDWIDE.

> "When I started on Disneyland, my wife used to say,
> 'But why do you want to build an amusement park?
> They're so dirty.' I told her that was just the point –
> mine wouldn't be." - Walt Disney

It was Buzz! The legendary Harrison "Buzz" Price, a consultant to Walt Disney, coined the term Imagineering in the 1950s for the creative group that still creates magic for the Walt Disney Company.

On opening day, Oct. 2, 1971, general admission was $3.50 per person at Walt Disney World. An 11 ride ticket cost an extra $5.75. In spring 2007, the cost to enter the park and ride all the rides, including tax, was $67!

Jennings Osborne's spectacular Walt Disney World Christmas light exhibit originated from his 1993 home display, which had 3 million lights and was so bright it could be seen by planes flying 80 miles away!

Using artificial-intelligence research to chart a course through the Magic Kingdom at Walt Disney World, 45-year old Rich Vosburgh was able to ride each of the 41 operating rides, attractions and shows in a record 10 hours, 40 minutes!

Check index, starting on page 105 for location of parks and attractions featured throughout this book.

Carousels

Cedar Point's popular Cedar Downs racing carousel was moved to the park from Cleveland's Euclid Beach when that park closed in 1969.

The Worlds' Largest Carousel can be found at the House on a Rock attraction in Spring Green, Wis. Built in 1981, the 36-ton machine is 35 feet tall, has 20,000 lights and contains 269 hand carved carousel animals. There's not one horse among them!

At 10-cents per ticket, a ride on the Central Park (N.Y.) Carousel in 1870 cost nearly as much as a working class man made in an hour!

MORE WOODEN CAROUSEL FIGURES WERE CARVED IN PHILADELPHIA THAN ANYWHERE ELSE IN THE U.S. !

The
RIVERVIEW
CAROUSEL,
NOW LOCATED AT
SIX FLAGS OVER
GEORGIA, ATLANTA,
WAS BUILT IN 1908 FOR RIVERVIEW PARK IN CHICAGO.
WHILE THERE IT WAS RIDDEN BY AL CAPONE,
WILLIAM RANDOLPH HEARST, AND PRESIDENT WARREN G.
HARDING, AMONG OTHERS.

BELIEVE IT OR NOT!
THE "CARROUSEL" AT HERSHEYPARK
WAS SPELLED WRONG BY THE ORIGINAL SIGN PAINTER— AND NOBODY HAS CHANGED THAT SPELLING TO THIS DAY!

English carousels are also known as gallopers or roundabouts.

English carousels turn clockwise, while American carousels turn counter-clockwise.

Various names have been used by carousel manufacturers through the years to describe their rides, including Carrousel, Carousel, Carousell, Carrousell, Carousselle, Carousele, Carrousele, Caroussel, Carousal, Carossel, Carry-Us-All, Flying Horses, Merry-Go-Round, Riding Gallery, and Roundabout.

Caro-Seuss-EL

is the
name of the merry-go-round

AT UNIVERSAL'S ISLANDS OF ADVENTURE
THAT FEATURES COLORFUL CHARACTERS
FROM THE DR. SEUSS BOOKS, INCLUDING—
COWFISH FROM McELLIGOTT'S POOL, AND
THE TWIN CAMELS FROM ONE FISH, TWO FISH.

POP ARTIST
ANDY WARHOL
WAS A COMPULSIVE AND PASSIONATE COLLECTOR
OF CAROUSEL HORSES!

*Check index, starting on page 105 for location of parks
and attractions featured throughout this book.*

Ferris Wheels

George Ferris's wheel, while not the first vertical passenger wheel, was certainly the largest, the most highly engineered, and the most spectacular. It also had the greatest impact on pleasure wheel history.

Ferris's wheel had 36 cars, each the size of a small streetcar which held up to 60 riders. It took 20 minutes to make a complete revolution.

During its 19 weeks of operation at the 1893 Columbian Exposition, nearly 1.5 million people paid 50-cents each to ride the Ferris wheel.

Believe It or Not! At 264 feet tall, the original Ferris wheel was taller than any building that existed at the time – anywhere in the world!

Check index, starting on page 105 for location of parks and attractions featured throughout this book.

THE ORIGINAL **FERRIS WHEEL**, WHICH DEBUTED ON JUNE 21 AT THE 1893 WORLD'S COLUMBIAN EXPOSITION IN CHICAGO, WAS BUILT BY GEORGE WASHINGTON FERRIS, A CIVIL ENGINEER AND BRIDGE BUILDER FROM PITTSBURGH.

GRAZIANO

Once it closed at the Columbian Exposition in Chicago, the Ferris wheel operated at the 1904 Louisiana Purchase Exposition in St. Louis before it was sold for scrap in 1905.

The 7-Year Wheel

It took W.E. Sullivan, owner of the Eli Bridge Company seven years to design and build his first portable wheel. The 45-foot tall Big Eli wheel premiered on May 23, 1900 in Central Park, Jacksonville, Ill., grossing $5.56 for the day!

It took seven years to design and build the $50 million, 443-foot tall London Eye, which opened March 1, 2000 and gave rides to 3.5 million people its first year!

The most unusual looking Ferris wheel ever created operated at the US Rubber exhibit at the 1964 New York World's Fair – it was an 80 foot wheel disguised as a giant rubber tire!

Located on the south bank of the River Thames, The 443-foot tall London Eye provides more rides than any Ferris wheel in the world – over 4 million each year!

The original design for Ferris's wheel was first drawn in 1891 at an engineer's banquet – on a napkin!

The Eli Bridge Company, builders of Ferris wheels since 1893, has only built one bridge in its history!

George Ferris died in 1896 of typhoid fever - only 3 years after his groundbreaking ride premiered. He was 37 years old and in financial ruin!

A Wheel Experience

The 150 foot tall Wonder Wheel at Coney Island's Deno's Wonder Wheel Park, is one of the most unusual Ferris wheels ever built. Eight of its gondolas travel in the traditional manner as the wheel turns, but as it rotates, 16 additional gondolas slide back and forth on rails from the outer to the inner rims creating an entirely different wheel experience!

The idea of a pleasure wheel dates back to written descriptions of such rides in Russia and England – nearly four centuries ago.

The 443-foot tall London Eye is the most expensive Ferris wheel ever built - $50 million!

Japan's first Ferris wheel which opened at the 1906 Osaka Victorious Fair – was powered by a steam engine!

The BIGGEST WHEEL in the WORLD!

The ferris wheel used at Earl's Court, London
was a quarter of a mile around - 300 feet across -
and carried 1600 passengers.

93

THE PACIFIC WHEEL

GRAZ

AT PACIFIC PARK ON THE SANTA MONICA (CALIFORNIA) PIER — IS THE ONLY **SOLAR-POWERED** FERRIS WHEEL IN THE WORLD!

Big Wheels Keep on Turning

At 525 foot tall, China's Star of Nanchang is the world's tallest wheel, besting the London Eye by 82 feet. That record will tumble during the first quarter of 2008 when the Singapore Flyer is set to open in Singapore, topping the Star of Nanchang by approximately 10 feet!

Gondolas in the shape of Mr. Potato Head, a Cabbage Patch kid, a Tonka Truck, and an M&M are among those on a 60 foot tall Ferris wheel INSIDE the Toys 'R' Us store in Times Square, NY.

Check index, starting on page 105 for location of parks and attractions featured throughout this book.

Food

William Morrison and John Wharton of Tennessee were awarded the first patent for a Cotton Candy machine in 1898. During the 1904 St. Louis World's Fair, the two sold more than 68,000 boxes of what they called "fairy floss" - for 25-cents each!

If every hotdog that Legoland Windsor sold each season were laid out end to end, they would circle the park four times – 13 miles!

Believe It or Not! During its heyday, the Shore Dinner Hall at Rocky Point Park could serve 3,000 people at one time. During the course of a summer weekend they would easily serve 15,000 meals that included 5,000 chickens, 1,700 pounds of French fries, and 10,000 gallons of chowder!

Check index, starting on page 105 for location of parks and attractions featured throughout this book.

GUESTS

AT SCHLITTERBAHN WATERPARK ANNUALLY USE MORE THAN ONE MILLION PACKETS OF KETCHUP, MUSTARD AND MAYONNAISE TO ENHANCE THEIR MAIN COURSES OF: 45,000 TURKEY LEGS, 90,000 SAUSAGES ON A STICK, 10 TONS OF HAMBURGER, 22 TONS OF CHICKEN STRIPS AND SEVEN MILES OF FOOT LONG CORN DOGS.

HOLIDAY WORLD, MAGIC SPRINGS AND LAKE COMPOUNCE OFFER **UNLIMITED** SOFT DRINKS TO ALL GUESTS — **FREE!**

In 2006, **10,450 candy apples** were sold at Carowinds – all hand made in the park's candy shop by the same person!

Hot Dog!

In 1874, a newspaper at Coney Island, NY, suggested that the meat in Charles Feltman's popular "red hots" was dog meat. Thanks to that editorial, the red hots were renamed and the American hot dog was born!

Feltman had created the specialty sausage earlier that year and was doing well selling them, but it was Nathan Handwerker who brought international fame to the sandwich. Nathan, then a Manhattan restaurant manager landed a job at Feltman's popular restaurant, and thanks to the fact that he could eat all the hot dogs he wanted for free, was able to save over $300 to start his own restaurant.

It is widely believed that entertainers Jimmy Durante and Eddie Cantor, who performed locally, were upset that Feltman had raised the price of his dogs to a dime and urged Nathan to go into business. He did so and rented a building nearby at the corner of Stillwell and Surf Avenue and in 1916 opened his own restaurant.

He sold hot dogs at five-cents each, half what Feltman was charging. Many of the passers-by were weary of any place that would sell such inexpensive food and most passed by Nathan's stand for the better-known Feltman's, located further down Surf Avenue. Using the island's spirit for inspiration Nathan hired bums to stand around the counter to give the impression he was busy, paying them in hot dogs. The crowds, seeing only unkempt patrons, still stayed away. Nathan then took the concept to the next level, had the bums clean themselves up and wear doctor's outfits so they looked well-off. A new sign erected above the establishment proclaimed, "If doctors eat our hot dogs, you know they're good!"

The Stillwell Avenue subway station opened a few years later and Nathan benefited from his location directly across from it on Surf Avenue. Crowds flocked to the new "Nickel Empire" and the simple stand grew into a full-scale service center with dozens of cashiers and long lines.

Burger & Coke Please! The 1950s-inspired restaurant chain, Johnny Rockets, will begin showing up in Six Flags parks during the summer 2007 season – with their dancing and singing employees, juicy burgers and their Oreo cookie milk shakes!

CHOC-A-LOT!

131,250 FIVE-POUND **HERSHEY** CHOCOLATE BARS WERE SOLD AT **HERSHEYPARK** IN 2006!

Knott's Berry Farm's first eatery, the Chicken Dinner Restaurant is still in business, seats more than 900 guests at a time, serves more than 1.5 million guests each year, and is the largest full-service chicken restaurant in California!

Legoland Windsor sells 1,282,000 ounces of ice cream each season – enough to fill 215 bathtubs to the very top!

Here chick chick chick. Knoebels Amusement Resort serves nearly 10,000 barbequed chickens each season, 2.25 miles of hot dogs, and in excess of 30 tons of hamburger!

Check index, starting on page 105 for location of parks and attractions featured throughout this book.

Index

John Graziano *(ILLUSTRATOR, PICTURED RIGHT)* is only the fifth person to take up the pen as the official illustrator for Ripley`s Believe It or Not! Prior to joining the Ripley team in 2004, and following his education at the Newark School of Fine and Industrial Arts and the Art Institute of Pittsburgh, John designed trading card sets and a portrait series based on the 1960s cult TV show "Dark Shadows." He has also created comic strips for "Scream Queens" magazine, sculpted figures that have been made into wax museum pieces, provided book illustrations, designed t-shirt graphics and created storyboards and concept drawings for Hollywood films. John is a bass player and vocalist in a 1960s tribute band appropriately called "60`s Groove."

Tim O'Brien *(AUTHOR, PICTURED LEFT)*, VP Publishing & Communications for Ripley Entertainment, is responsible for coordinating the publicity and promotion of the company's 60-plus attractions throughout the world. Prior to his position with Ripley, Tim served 18 years as senior editor of *Amusement Business,* the world's leading business magazine for the amusement park and attraction industries. Since becoming an industry specialist more than two decades ago, the award winning photojournalist has had more than 5,000 articles and 3,000 photos printed and has had 11 books published, seven of which chronicle the amusement industry. His previous two books, both published by Ripley Publishing are *The Wave Maker – The Story of Theme Park Pioneer George Millay* (2004), and *Legends – Pioneers of the Amusement Park Industry* (2006).

CPSIA information can be obtained
at www.ICGtesting.com
Printed in the USA
FFOW03n0750270217
32891FF